JULIEANN C

MILK TEETH

POEMS

GUILDHALL PRESS

Published in May 2015

Guildhall Press
Unit 15
Ráth Mór Business Park
Derry
Ireland
BT48 0LZ
info@ghpress.com
www.ghpress.com
T: 028 7136 4413

Cover image © Paula Gillespie, 2015.

Cover design © David Campbell, 2015.

ISBN: 978 1 906271 97 8

Guildhall Press gratefully acknowledges the financial support of the Arts Council of Northern Ireland as a principal funder under its Annual Funding Programme.

Acknowledgements

This collection owes everything to others – to family, friends, colleagues and strangers – all those who ignite the spark. Thank you. My sincere thanks to Damian Smyth and the Arts Council of Northern Ireland for granting me an award under the Support for the Individual Artist Programme. Huge thanks to Paul, Peter, Joe, Kevin, Jenni and everyone at Guildhall Press for their optimism, sound advice, and for always having faith in me.

My thanks to my daughter, my mum, Susie, and brothers David, Peter, Alan and Pablo, and my wonderful circle of friends, especially Miss Starrs, my book buddy and proofreader. Thanks also to anyone who has published my work elsewhere, and to those who take the time to read it now.

A special mention is due to David Campbell and Paula Gillespie for their creativity and help with the cover design.

About the Author

Julieann Campbell was born in 1976 and lives in Derry with her five-year-old daughter Saffron. A former reporter for the *Derry Journal*, Julieann's poetry has been widely published and she won 1ˢᵗ place for a collection in Ireland's 2008 Charles Macklin Poetry Competition.

Fuelled by a family link, Julieann has worked alongside the Bloody Sunday Trust on various projects. In 2008, she co-edited *Harrowing of the Heart: The Poetry of Bloody Sunday* (Guildhall Press), which contained previously unseen local work alongside that of Seamus Heaney, Brian Friel and John Lennon, as well as contributing to *City of Music: Derry's Music Heritage* and *Wonderful World of Worders*, both by Guildhall Press.

Her first non-fiction book in 2012, *Setting the Truth Free: The Inside Story of the Bloody Sunday Justice Campaign* (Liberties Press, Dublin), won the 2013 Christopher Ewart-Biggs Memorial Prize. Julieann is currently Chair of the Bloody Sunday Trust.

A member of Derry Writers' Group, Julieann is also a facilitator of oral history and is currently writing the educational graphic novel *We Shall Overcome* for the Museum of Free Derry.

Milk Teeth is her first solo collection of poetry.

MILK TEETH

POEMS

Words can be like X-rays,
if you use them properly
– they'll go through anything.

Aldous Huxley
Brave New World

For Saffron

CONTENTS

Trapped in Videotape

My childhood's trapped in videotape.
Forgotten, confined to a celluloid fate
and gathering dust. Obsolete.

Inside those tired cases, my father lives.
His voice still echoes, though we cannot hear him.
He speaks and laughs, dances at family weddings
and no doubt curses at the cameraman.

Inside, my mother's years pass
with her wit preserved intact. She ages
with a matriarchal grace we can't help but admire,
Creasing, but never changing.

Inside, my brothers are perennial children
or awkward, stroppy teens, or dressed for Hallowe'en
and no doubt posing for the cameraman.

Inside, we matured, we grew up.
Before our own children came
and videos went.

A Box-load of Memoirs
(For Johnny Campbell 1920-2013)

His letters are scattered
all over my house. In every room,
cursive remnants piled up in drawers,
tucked into bookshelves,
or boxed with great haste
and placed up high in tidying fits.
Or when my mother pays a visit.

The precise, old-fangled style
that elderly gentlemen do so well.
Deliberate and slow, he thrived
in the well-ordered lines,
the elaborate allograph,
a fountain pen's flourishes.

His writing meant everything
in catharsis.

He never knew,
but I loved those letters.
I found solace in yesterday's parables,
old family yarns, on the cusp of forgotten.
Glimpses into a bygone Derry,
of black sheep, dark secrets and revelations,
war heroes lost to mustard gas.
All in total recall.

Memories from the brink of senescence
a window to his world.

I would like to have told him
of my late, spare hours buried deep
in those well-thumbed pages.
In tales of folk long gone, of community,
and adventure on the 'Bolie' and Top O' the Hill.
So he knew I cared.

From the earliest,
I saw myself in his words and humour.
I recognised his turn of phrase as my own,
and my father's too.
Those letters made me glad of my lineage,
an articulate inheritance.

When I could,
I typed out each one as it came,
adding just the gentlest editor's caress,
a sheen for the benefit of future clan.
So they would know him.

Gradually, it swelled and we treated it well.
We travelled to Derby for his 90th birthday and
sat a large box on his knee.
Happy Birthday from us, Grandad.
He peeked inside
to see his own face peering back
and sat silent, smiling,
slowly realising what this was.

Books, lots of books – too many to count.
For him, a box-load of memoirs.

Derry Writers' Group

The Writers' Group, though daunting,
seemed suddenly full of promise.

Gathered in a tiny room,
they sat with one communal aim.
Like minds and scribbled lines
so hastily denied, never good enough.

I had dreaded all of this,
introductions and first impressions.

Some semblance of eloquence
when I dare to speak aloud.

Admitting guiltily
why I came here tonight.
Surreal AA meeting, addicted to prose.
Drunk on vocabulary.

Awkwardness aside, this makes sense.
Though novice now, I need to know
where this might lead.

First step so cautiously taken.
Reach out towards an elusive guiding light
that might never shine my way.

With scarcely an introduction,
they accepted me as one of their own
and I sat quietly, listening.
Brave, among my own kind.

Morning's Promise

(The *Carpathia* – April 1912)

If you are there we are firing rockets,
urged Marconi operators in wireless rescue.
Dead air. Sent into the ether.
Dead calm. Gone to the depths.

From the *Carpathia*,
women sobbed and wailed at dawn.
Cast their eyes out towards
that vast, murderous ocean.
For husbands
who would never come.

Lifeboats tethered, gave up their few
watched by frozen clusters below.
Their cold greying faces
all masks of misery.

From the *Carpathia*,
lost children waited amid the chaos
for parents gone to sombre graves.
Mothers crumpled in ruins
knowing theirs were among the lost.

Displaced souls sent out their prayers
wrapped warm and wandering. Incoherent.
Petitioning God with no success
and never an absolution.

From the *Carpathia*,
they glimpsed the New York skyline
and grasped at lives anew.

The Old Firestation House

Remember how we squandered
a thousand or so nights, where
we sat around 'til cockcrow
and put the world to rights?

There were usually three of us, the
pineapple blonde, redhead and dark one.
Charlie's Angels – chasing on
against the scold of morning.

It was on nights such as this that
we first felt aversion to lights too bright,
the vulgar dawn. Wearing sunglasses at 3am.
We battled to extend the night, and then,
in daring, took tools to remedy it.

We chiselled away until debris caved in
and this house smiled. Its sash-window limbs,
sealed tight by careless paint, gave way
and spread their shuttered wings.

We watched as wooden giants drew first breath
and folded out to greet the 21st century.
We oiled their heavy iron arms and shook hands.
We nested in their castle keep, complete with moats,
occasionally, pulling boats.

They drowned out day
and we swam in the confines.

One About Coffee Jars
(For my daddy)

That smooth, shiny seal would remain
until school spewed me out.
And I arrived home, weary,
laden with too many textbooks.

You'd save it for me. Summoning me to the kettle,
handing me the coffee jar, wait for the pop.

The slow reveal, the initial pierce.
Then running a fingernail along the curve
to break its foil fortress.

Here comes the potent, smoky aroma,
still I can smell it – subtle intake of breath.
Fill all the senses at once.

Coffee doesn't smell the same anymore.

And never have I felt that satisfying pop
without imagining you here.

Bygones
(Ode to a Fellow Poet)

I put you on a pedestal –
you stole it.

I offered you the world –
you hurled it back with a venom
I shall never comprehend.

No more I'll ask.

Though catalyst for much,
you failed in the basic humanity
demanded of a suitor.
Failed in all the promises made,
in love created.

You desecrated.

An affront to romance, that's you.
Cupid hangs his head in shame,
Eros knows you took his name in vain,
Keats wants his words back.

Crawford Square

On the way home
we stole into the glade.
No conventional glade, no Camelot,
simple sliver of grass in a bustling town.

Listed buildings loomed on all sides.
Victorian hedgerows
now so tall, they stoop
to kiss lush green below.

Drunk on romance and Buckfast
we peered through bushes like giddy explorers.
Finding holes in the shrubbery,
you helped me climb inside.
Secret garden, just us, the stars,
and Mother Earth.

I surrendered my favourite suede coat,
now Oxfam's finest,
upon which we lay, and you made love to me.
Then we slept.
Waking like Guinevere and Lancelot
under cloak of night.

The Atomium

The train carriage was almost empty,
another lonely trek across country. Another commute
from here to there with scarcely a word spoken.

Then I saw her again. In the distance, towering
high above the cityscape, the silvery Atomium stood.
Dominating my skewed horizon.

Futuristic beacon, sign of modern times,
I heard her troubled sigh from here, reminding me
of what once passed beneath her metallic orbs.

I saw it all again. Flashing past
as swiftly as the countryside outside my window.
Those space-age spheres whispered consolation,
of youth, of death, of what was not to be.

A young, impulsive love. Wind in our hair,
the motorbike roaring around her giant frame.
Now only I survive to recount the tales
we swore we'd not forget.

Has it really been so long?
Since summertime had meaning,
since your voice sent me reeling,
long-since silenced.

Outcasts

The oddest omen
presented one day in biting gale.

In coastal winds that sting the eyes
and batter the bones, he came to me.
Omen or coincidence, I felt the reaper smile.
The Gods conspiring.

Only the most hardened of smokers
would brave the north's arctic squall
on days like these.

He shuffled over,
sat close for body heat, and lit up.
Kind eyes now cloudy
– you could tell he'd been handsome once.
Now brittle, bent and curved
'round a walking stick.

We are outcasts, the lot of us,
he mused. *Great day for it.*
I have lung cancer
and find no peace to smoke anywhere.
We're done with!

I would face the wrath of earth if habit said so.

They thought I would die.
I said it's not the fags, it's the WIFE that's killing me.
Two heart attacks, the brain haemorrhage,
and now cancer – I think she's bad luck!

The haemorrhage was a funny one.
Once I woke up and pretended I didn't know her,
told her to put on her clothes and get out.
How I laughed.
She even rang the son, but I confessed.

With that he rose, bent in two by the wind.
Eyes lost in a friendly grimace.
That's my lift now, bye.
He pulled his coat close, braced, and went on.

I stubbed out my roll-up and vowed to quit again.

Still We Shine

(For Mama Cass)

Since school, we drew close and held fast,
a pair of dizzy magnets destined to attract.
She shined and I fell in behind.

She was the brains of the class, one of the gifted few,
I was the sleepy one with sleeves deemed too long
and a slack to my step. Full of big ideas,

still we drew together.
Her ample garden had two big statue lions
that led to a lawn, stretching out like a Jane Austen novel,
while mine led to a lively council estate,

still we drew together.
Her father was on the school's Board of Governors,
mine was an erudite 'sticky' cab driver
with a big 1970s' moustache. Worlds apart,

still we drew together.
Everything changed when I made her that mix-tape.
The Doors, Pixies, Velvet Underground and more,
all the stuff I'd hoped she'd adore. She did.

Soon we sought big boots and Barbarella dresses.
We bloomed and multiplied as a century's quarter passed,
and, though rock and roll faded, our star never has.

Still she shines and I fall in behind.

You, Me and Dylan Thomas

Hidden now from all the chaos.
Friday traffic. Deadlines and raised voices.

Reality drowned out
by the relentless, rushing waves
still quite audible
through flimsy, love-soaked walls.
You and I. Familiar navy sky.

Escape from the strains of the city.
Seeking a solitude in nature's rhythm,
in its soothing celestine effect.

When night finally fell, we smoked
and felt the surf crash about us.

Perched on a lonely rock, we talked.
Seeing each other through velvet darkness,
faintly visible, but only to ourselves.

Caravan by Culdaff's unspoilt edge,
we warmed. Observing Neptune's kingdom.

Content in everything, we saw
night's unending darkness broken
by an occasional deliberate flash.
The reassuring lighthouse
– I think you called it.

Click, click, cutting through the blackness.
Keeping us constant company.

Last hours now.
I sit by the unsteady table, scribbling,
you lie out on our makeshift bed with Dylan Thomas.
Raindrops pummel the sides, roof, waters ahead.
Quietly comforting,
like when we were young.

Last Man Standing
(For John)

He cut a lonely figure into the landscape.
Among so many; standing tall; afraid to fall,
in need of embrace, or friendly face.

My soul reached out.
His ordeal, my worst nightmare.
Surviving a sibling,
last man standing.

Nonchalant,
putting on a brave face.

Waving You Away

Tuesday's cold evening air
held an eerie feeling, prophetic almost.

Stifling emotion as I wave you away,
in place of another. Temporary mother.

*

Exaggerated waves, just as she might,
until the car lights disappear from sight.

Until I am but a speck of dust
in your rear-view mirror.

You smile – craning your neck to see.
Me – animated to the last.

*

Waving you off, just as she did me.
But this time it's different.

This time I wave you away
to a bright new shiny life, far from home.

No more term-time farewells –
you flee the nest with our blessing.

*

On this occasion, she will return,
take up the mantle once more.

But someday, someday …
Someday
I will carefully prepare packed lunches,
arrange your things as I did tonight.
Someday
I will do this in her place.
Someday
her absence will not be a leisurely one
and I quake at the thought.

Flashes of future tense
tear as they slip past.

When I hurt just like a mother would,
and I felt just like a mother should.

Waving you away.

Waterloo Road

On Waterloo Road, we came.
Found ourselves in each other.
On the windowsill of
a slick, primary coloured Travelodge.
On form, laid out on basic bedding.
Rampant, exposed.

On Tower Bridge, we kissed.
Blinded in swirling, cotton blizzard,
mouths warm and velvety.
Blind to our skin-deep saturation.
Our own infatuation.

On the Underground, we marvelled
at each other, at the long darkness beyond,
our giggling reflections within.

On Southbank, we twirled in narcotic haze.
Weaving a dance through the Tate's sapling trees,
all shimmery, dressed in tiny snow-diluted lights.

We faded. We lost. We may have died,
but our souls dance there still.

Lucy, Sky, Diamonds

Ordinarily of moderate mind,
last night
I dipped my toes in the pool of excess.

Confident of my sanity,
I pushed the boat out.

Cast into the unknown.
Now reaping
the rewards of such illumination.

Yesterday's crescent moon gives way.
Afternoon gleam.

Still I remain
cocooned in this most treasured state.
Enchanted by a haze, unwittingly created.

Holding with a childlike grasp –
the strings of sleep.

A Crime in Any Language

Deliciate: Verb. To feast upon,
to indulge in feasting, to luxuriate, to enjoy oneself.

Since I first heard it, it stuck fast.
I like to roll it around my tongue
with all the swelled sweetness of a gobstopper.

Deliciate … I feast upon it, and quietly despair
that someone, in their wisdom, decided
to remove it from the dictionary.

Gone. Extinguished. While words with no flavour
furrow deep and take up residence. *Amazeballs*,
selfie, *twerk*, *vlog*, *mahoosive*. Let me despair,
just a little.

A Child (Or the Lack Thereof)

Tonight I love you more.
A love that threatens to burst its banks,
engulf me in its heaving swell.

Tonight I love you more.
Circumstance brought us here
and soon will pass, but *love*,
love will last. Flourishing.

This, too, will end. This sorrow
shall bring sweet relief in time.
But tonight I love you more
because you are mine.

x

Come Out of Hiding

Emerge cautiously under darkness.
Weak with trepidation –
and weak with defeat.

We drove in silence.
Past midnight, late enough for none to see
this broken shell surrounding.

Winding roads as empty as this womb.
Still pushing out all it considers waste,
expelling it naturally; quietly.

We question cruellest nature,
a biological efficiency all too clear.
I curse this finely tuned machine I call my own.

Staring vacantly as streets flashed by unnoticed.
Once hopeful, now sullied, sickened
to feel this slow, deliberate trickle of rejection.

All that blossoming life inside, redundant.
Failure in procreation, humanity's basic aim.
He holds my hand throughout.

Cast out. I shiver, remembering all.
Stains of miscarriage still taunt from new sheets,
refusing to fade, like motherhood has.

St Patrick's Night (Revised)

Unsettled under neon lights,
we sipped our drinks with anxious breath.
Weak vodka sat uneasy in the throat.

A foreboding not even disco could soothe.
A sobering disturbance in the Force
while all were drenched in beer,
and staggering in green.

Calls I never thought I'd have to make.
Perched on the edge of the armchair in Mossy,
knowing it must be done, it must be said,
despite the rising dread.
Utter aloud *our father is dead*.

One brother was jovial, mid-higgyback,
he laughed out loud and gasped for air.
Put her down a wee minute, pup,
I need to talk to you.

The others followed suit, one by one.
Crushed, they came running, and I seem to recall
anguished fists took on the sturdy back gate
and lost.

Ten years ago tonight, so soon the years forget.
Perched there and petrified,
a dialler of doom, complicit in death.
I remember it all. Yet nothing.

Galway Whispers

No-one saw us slip away mid-celebration.
While newlyweds cut up the dance floor, circled
by beer-bouncing, glossy, groomed guests
all claps and cheers and smiles.

Nobody noticed us return, faces flushed, or
saw as we slid back into our seats.
Salvaging our glasses, we drank deep.
All giggles and secret glances.

No-one knew we had just made history. Not even you.
But I felt it happen. A muted lightning bolt
as something clicked within my abundant body.
A gentle nudge to hint at an arrival.

That night, danced out and sprawled on hotel sheets,
I whispered quietly in your ear: *Are you awake?*
You turned to me and smiled, on the cusp of sleep,
You know, I think we made a baby.

Happy New Year

Never made mention of it then,
this symptom of an ever-changing culture.

No more letters, no more phone calls.
The usual intimacy replaced by an army
of mechanical messengers.
The modern phenomena: text message.

This wizardry, this marvel
of the 21st century
became all too clear, countdown to twelve,
to the first hour of a new year.

All faces downwards, captivated.
Gadgets now telling of true sentiment
as countless millions stop dead
to type their words of welcome.

Useless now, these pleasantries of the past.
Now all we need are tiny machines,
capable of prose, if the writer should will it so.
Capable of spanning ocean, if the sender send it so.

Networks jammed. Still,
so many arms empty of embrace.
All come to a standstill,
ushering in the New Year
with their thumbs.

The Day We Brought Her Home

She slept,
and we, though sleep deprived,
blinkered by our unreal domain,
sat squat on the end of the bed.

Knees folded in, cocooned into balls,
we sat soundlessly, watching. On high alert
afraid to move, lest this tiny thing stirred
and we had to start all over again.

The soothe, the sway, lullabies with no words
just the distant, comforting hummmm
felt in tired brains, remote yet reverberating
like a heartbeat in a headstand.

She slept,
and we, still too fearful to give in, sat wired,
watching her chest softly rise, softly fall,
keeping count of each fledgling breath.

Doll in a Moses basket, we dared
not look away. We sat there for hours,
hypnotised by her every sound, every shift.
We sat, weak and scared for tomorrow,
seeing in the glow of morning.

Mother and Child

From nothing
I grasped the fundamentals.
Fell headfirst into the mothering way
and emerged smiling.

Life lessons learned.
Tricks, now passed down to me.
She instructed in the simplest tasks,
and step by patient step,
showed me the way.

Crash course
in the nuances of motherhood.
Gratefully, I listened,
flourishing at the closeness.

She reigns supreme.
Reluctant master of all she surveys,
the vast shell in which she dwells
now widowed too young.

Now I see with crystal clarity,
she has been preparing me for this role
my whole life.

A challenge I now accept.
A baton I hold high, and
race towards the future.

The *Derry Journal*

Sent on fetching errand,
I lose myself in the *Journal*'s
hallowed File Room.

Nestled among centuries
of cold, yellowing paper,
I am carried away.
Row after row of treasure
piled ceiling high.

Newspapers tell the city's tale
in dusty decades, since 1772.
The grandeur of a bygone era,
the attention to detail.

A rich fluency of language
long-since forgotten.
Dumbed down, simplified,
forgotten by time.

We are but custodians
tasked with sustaining this trove.
To pass it on, protect it.
Willing, I delve headfirst
into the annals of Derry.

(I hold in my hands *your* history)

The earliest papers
have long-since disappeared.
Pillaged over the years,
ripped from their binding
and mislaid forever.

Liberated from
their lonely resting place
long before our time.

Perhaps by a succession
of editors or reporters – ancestors
who lost themselves in this room
just as I do now.

Taking something of worth
upon their departure.

Two-hundred-year-old
masterpieces, now someone's
mantelpiece folly.

Someone Still Remembers You

(It had escaped my notice until then)

'You said *thank you kindly*!
You know, your father used to say that too –
I haven't heard it in years!'

Exclamation with booming voice,
beaming smile through bright red lipstick, then
she flounced back to her deaths and classifieds.

Still, the sun shone and the air felt light,
I gave a knowing smile to the heavens,
grateful for the slightest signs
when we least expect them.

Someone still remembers you.

Maternity Leave of Senses

I fear it most of all –
the milk diminishing and she,
no longer needing me.

All that newness slipping away,
bundle now bouncing
and wise to us all.

Mischief in the making, she glows.
All the first times, learning curves
that leave me dizzy and wanting more.

Maternity leave of senses.
What if I never feel this fervour again?
Perhaps this was my first and last time,
last few drops, last tingles.

The contours of her face from that angle.
The milk-white tiny hands, clinging in instinct,
and me, all hormone-infused, infatuated.

The Relief of Derry

We were there for the disgrace,
for the great lie exposed.
So many rusty bloodstains,
tarnished names – now exalted.

Thousands stood in solidarity,
squinting in the rare, most welcome sun
of Guildhall Square.
Rays glittering like hopes
off its newly laid granite.

We needed to be there.
Among friends, they said
through loudspeakers.

The city's breath hung heavy.
A palpable fear, full of nervousness,
full of guilty excitement.

We watched the hands of the city clock
play chase. Countdown to truth,
to Cameron's belated bleat.
Waiting patiently for any sign of life
through stained-glass windows.

We were there
for truth revealed in gestures,
cheered by all below.

Thumbs-up of a good report
beamed around the world,
with a city's vindication.

Not just any names.
Our names.
Our people.

Rapturous crowds
saw Widgery torn apart.
Tossed aside,
consigned to history's dustbin.
Its insult now
fluttering in the wind.

We were there for grave admissions.
Unjustified and unjustifiable, he said.
Wrong, he said.

We all became lighter
as decades of weight fell away
and fact replaced fiction.

Lord Saville saw the relief of Derry.
Though flawed, he did try,
and we breathe easier.

The Lazy Virus

Seriously, tell me –
when did grammar
become so unfashionable
that words shrank away
to be replaced
by this *text speak*?

Who sat at home, busy
inventing these infuriations?

I laugh at your LOLs, and
seethe at the OMGs sown too freely
by PPL who should know better.
Gee, aren't shortcuts GR8?
Jury's out.
I'll decide L8R.

Like a lazy virus, it spreads
and slowly stifles imagination
to choke our lexicon.
Bastardising the language
for a quick fix.

Milk Teeth

In finding myself, I first had to find you,
and thrust into this pearly, clinical world, it began.

Placed on my chest, you murmured
while we cried through words of welcome.

You, the delicate expression of our infatuation,
eyes wide as saucers and questioning all.
You, the fusion who brings music to these walls
in melodious infant babble.

I shall show you the world and how it works
to make your passage easier.

As a listening ear, I will hear when you call
and comfort in hushed, measured tone.
I will heal with myriad kisses and instruct you
in the ways of others less loving.

Tiny flower, you bloom and hold the best of us
in perfect synthesis.

Runaway year, you no longer cling to me, and
as the swell subsides, so does the worry.
My body relents. No longer lactating
at the mere thought of lips curled to meet me.

Instead, I fear the nip of milk teeth,
still tiny bumps but budding with potential.
Instead, I wean, and indulge in that indistinct scent
that lingers long after you do.

I cut my teeth with your arrival.
Now embedded, you thrive and we catch you.

Oh, Velveteen

Braving the weeds
and newly spun webs,
we catch the scarce, moonless hours.

We have discovered the joy
in planetary pleasures. The infinite sky.

Warmer nights favour this new hobby,
still we huddle, captivated,
out the back lane, cast
no shadows in pitch darkness.

Tea steaming and ready,
we wrap up, Miss Starrs and I,
(Starry by name, starry by nature)
and, venturing out into the frigid air,
unleash her split-new telescope.
Emblazoned down one side,
its name, the mighty *Astromaster*.

What a sight. One could stargaze forever
and still not skim the surface.

Countless starry glints
in velveteen suffice. Still,
they are no match for the moon.
Bulbous, magnificent
and tantalisingly close.

We count craters by the dozen,
expecting to see the US flag
just as Aldrin and Armstrong left it.

But Saturn, most of all. She enthrals.

Microscopic amber sphere,
so delicate and shrouded, she sparkles.
Caught up in the invisible veins of space
then pierced by an arrow.
Distinct, cartoon-like,
and light years away.

With August, a new friend arrived.
God of gas – unmistakable Jupiter.
The four moons orbiting
lay trail across its glittering belt.
From here, she appears to spin.

And momentarily, as the eye focuses,
Jupiter's red stripe flashes and is gone again.

Bauble on a Christmas tree,
she hangs there, suspended.
Watching us so far below,
each starstruck.

Aberystwyth
(In search of Paul Davis)

I had arrived
at its grand Victorian station,
and, stepping outside, burst into tears
at the sight of his hometown.

Too silent a taxi drive
through inky, winding streets
left me here a stranger.

A crash of deafening waves
took me by surprise
as did its pastel-pretty terraced seafront
curving around Cardigan Bay.

The hotel room was too small, too white,
so I walked the promenade.
Past rainbow terraces, arcades, hotels,
following the coast as far as I could.
I found a castle, and cursed my negligence
at not telling him I loved him still.

Effort discarded, old friend. Letters lost to routine.
Real life intervened, and we left it too late.
I sat on a beach pavilion and cried
for years that ran away with us.

Knowing I should have done more,
written more, loved more.

Imagining he once sat there too,
I hear his voice, *sweetness*, *cherub*,
never by name, but soaked with affection.

Giving into sleep, I dreaded the slow walk
to the morning's crematorium, and
thanked all that brought him to me.

All God's Creatures

She has no fear.
Displays a remarkable regard
for all things non-human,
set on befriending every one.

Dogs, cats, arachnids, rats,
all earn an introduction,
Hello, my name is Haffron.
Never minding
that they don't reply.

A precise fascination,
absorbed in all God's creatures.
A joy so readily lost in adulthood, when,
as pests, they are swatted away.

Scooping up the tiniest things,
she lets them loose to crawl, flitting
like dust particles up and down her arm.
She calls tiny flies bees,
and flees for cover.

She entraps horror-film spiders,
only to christen each Charlotte
and implore they spin webs.
Sometimes they do.

Fuelled by curiosity,
she tiptoes after daddy longlegs,
hell bent on conversation,
where we just pulled the legs off
and watched them hop.

Chime

Chime, such a pretty word.
It falls from my tongue in musical notes
and hangs, pregnant, in mid-air,
packed with promises.

From the back door, I often still to listen
as the bells of St Eugene's sing to me.
Each chime a cathedral's choir, sent to soothe
its citizens, diffusing through the air.

Rolling unwanted cigarettes
just to savour the moment, a reason to linger,
intent on hearing every peal,
every glorious, love-spun wedding.

At year's end, I stood there again.
Arctic chill whistled around my legs
and escaped through to the hearth.

Come 20:13pm, every bell in the city
resounded at once. A cacophony
of churches, cathedrals, town halls
rang as one, heralding
a City of Culture.

Grand pyrotechnics fell in behind
– a sky full of fireworks and ambition.
Ring in with wonder so many cultures,
a city awakening.

Last night, the breeze sang again.
The Angelus had passed,
so what was the occasion?

Then all was clear
– white smoke had appeared,
serenading us of a new Pope.
The Vatican's birth of new hope
carried to us in isobars.

I wonder how I could possibly live elsewhere
when, here, the night air sings to me.

Epiphany

Oh, solitude,
you could be the best friend
I have ever met.

The wisest decision,
the natural conclusion
to a love story bereft
of romance.
You, my lonely evening
spent smoking, thinking,
by the back door.

My empty bed,
my empty head.
Climb out.
Flee the what-ifs, run.

What if I'd carried on.
What if we were wrong
and passion died, taking us with it?

What if I lived long, craving more
and couldn't ignore?
What if I stumble on alone
from here. From us.

Would you let me?
You did.

Wait a While Longer

Ears pricked for the slightest murmur,
fine-tuned to danger, an alertness
coyote-quick, just in case …

She's right, again.
Outgrown all our precautions,
and though I protest – she now talks louder.

Out go fluffy blankets, bibs, first toys.
Tonight, down comes the safety gate.
Dismantled, and thus ends her infancy.

Indignant at remnants of baby things,
she rebels. Everything goes in demands.
Except for pink, everything pink.

Sleep eludes me. Motherhood too.
Or at least the first tentative steps
that brought us here and changed everything.

Ears pricked to her every breath,
I'll wait a while longer …

A Sea of Shoes
(In Their Footsteps campaign)

Tiny pink shoes, they speak volumes.
Empty of feet, they flutter
down 10 Downing Street's pavement
as though they are dancing.

A handwritten note dances alongside:
I was five months old when we were blown up
in the 1974 Dublin bombings.
We never stood a chance.

Men's size-10 brogues, they speak volumes.
Lining the street outside the Ministry of Defence,
the stark, unpolished shoes of every man.
Their once-proud owners slain
in a war not of their making.

Murdered by British soldiers,
he was a much-loved son and brother.
Loved today more than yesterday,
but never as much as tomorrow.

Elsewhere, decadent cowboy boots
catch the eye of Belfast's passers-by.
Worn that night, they scream for justice.

I am a Miami Showband Massacre survivor,
my three Miami brothers were murdered
at Banbridge, July 1975.

Truth is the first casualty of war
and the last prisoner to be released.

Memory-Foam Home

God bless this memory-foam home,
where the outlines of yesterday persist
with no fear for intervening years. Prevailing

around every corner, faint reminders, traces
of full days lived within, the banter, the laughter,
festive gatherings and fistfights. Every

room in which tears were shed, snowballing
first kisses, or broken hearts, or in defiance
of rulebooks and reason. Fragments

of us trail behind. Here we are forever little children,
or teenaged and torn, wishing for adulthood,
though now long flown the coop. Even

now a ghost inhabits that worn-out old armchair
that's been through the wars and begs
for an end to its misery. Watermarks

of time, sentient limbs of a family tree,
and counting its branch whorls, I thrill to see
the ripening. Feeling all of my 38 years.

Pablo's Part

Riot scene, feign fury for the Army,
rubber bricks and polystyrene barricades,
a camaraderie of sorts. Until the big scene.

Overwhelmed, he hid his anxiety well,
actually acted out that fabled family tale.
He quietly complied –
becoming someone else, for just a while.
His false bravado not fooling anyone.

Hours later, as we nursed our well-earned drinks,
I wiped a touch of grime from his collar,
without thinking, and glimpsing remnants
of the fake blood, he quietly caved in.
Swiftly broken, let the façade fall.

You Need to Know
(Dear Mum)

You need to know
you've been everything.

My mother, my teacher,
my conscience and friend.

Do not doubt
all I am is because of you.

Mocking Clocks

Past midnight –
the kitchen's oversized mocking clock
makes sport of me.
Illuminates the obvious.

Though not yet grown,
I meet middle-age head-on.

Intent.
Deathly defiant, gritted
but lacking that which means most –
a hand to hold.

Late thirties.
You'd think time would take me
in creases and crisis.
You'd think time
would
sting
more,
not come and go
like an occasional guest.

Fleeting.
So full of what-ifs.
A tired, rambling mind –
but the stories,
oh, the stories I shall tell.

Past midnight – three hours past in fact.
As these final lines come slow
and take root.

       Knowing
by morning, I'll be a woman.

The Bigger Picture Prevails

These sprawling streets and houses beckon me.
Regardless of where I roam, where instinct leads
the bigger picture prevails.

Across the S-shaped bridge with watery eyes,
caught in the realisation, the quiet, swelling pride.
Here I am – home again.

The Foyle's meander seduces my sight –
leads me yet further upstream, beyond
its dusk-cloth of lights, beyond the tide.

Knowing I'll feel forever welcome here.
Recurring laughter in the strangest of places,
kindness in the strangest of faces.

A thousand familiar sights,
sea of endless, twinkling lights.
Make this city shine. Make this city mine.

Christmas Eve

Silly really

the absurd routines ingrained in us
when no-one was watching.
Little habits that make me laugh now.

Lining the stairs in order of rank
to see if Santa's been.
Bleary eyed but itching to descend,
waiting faithfully as elders take the helm.
March on, Campbell family.

The day we closed my father's coffin,
we stood there again.
Eldest first, we waited in line,
one at a time.
We felt deep the poignant stab
as our surviving elder took the helm.

Silly really.

Freefalling

(For Felix Baumgartner)

His mother
watched him fall from space,
and no doubt masked the terror rising
when he began to spin in freefall.

Millions watched him
abandon all in livestream
to shatter world records.
Stepping out into
earth's cobalt curve
on the edge of space.

Let go. Falling faster
than the speed of sound.
Plunging into orbit,
freefalling
into school textbooks,
into the stuff of legend.

A thousand miles away,
I sat transfixed, poker-straight on a sofa,
and shared tears with his mother
as he took back control in descent.

Together, we punched the air,
and squealed aloud
when he landed – alive –
and hit the ground running.

Jim Upstairs

This ancient, echoing house has seen the unthinkable,
expiring life, mere yards from where I lie.
Death beckoning above my head,
above this very bed,
and I did not hear the scythe.

Last breaths unnoticed. Last Rites denied
while the city baked in clammy heatwave.
Beyond his walls and windows, we saw nothing.
Despite his priesthood, his blessed devotion,
lying alone and dying alone.
Only the Almighty for company.

Just once, these solid concrete walls lost their charm.
Nobody heard him cry. Heard him die
nor sought him out thereafter.
Absence gone unnoticed
until they found him where he fell.

Then the Company Phones Arrived

Sleek black plastic threat, I see
I must keep my distance. Regard you from afar,
like the enemy you are.

All boxed and new, you gleam.
An idle menace sent to frustrate, to intimidate.
I stand firm, glaring through cautious eye.

I refuse your advances
as you lay siege to my senses.
Cower at your pocket-sized
confidence. *Look at me, all shiny.*

Arms held close, hands recoiled
and clammy – as though any minute
you'll snap up and take chunks from me.
Or sting like the back-lane nettles
I can never avoid.

I care nothing for your handiness,
your tricks or technical brilliance.
I won't adore your Apps, whatever they may be.
It's a whole new language I barely understand,
and have no wish to.

They may laugh,
with their nimble fingers all a-frenzy.
I'd laugh too, if this wasn't so serious.
Thrust into an inevitable future
and far from ready.

While I can, I wage a war that we are losing.

Lie Long
(The Farmer's Son)

Lie long, until dawn came
and fell again. Until birdsong
ceased with dusk
and we descended
into ourselves.

I lay flushed, naked,
star-shaped in flannel sheets.
Struck with the malaise
only passion brings.

You rose early to feed the cattle.
Donning old rags, happed up warm
and stole out to greet the morning.
Tend the land with well-worn hand.

Lie long, you returned,
slipped silently beneath, and
into the warmth, into my arms.

You Said We Were Stardust
(The Soldier's Son)

Guilty secret –
lurk in murky corners.
I dare not speak of you aloud
for fear of ridicule.

They were right.
We, so wrong, so foolish to leap
into the night, into the cosmos.

It began at the Natural History Museum.
Cooing over meteorites and moon rock,
caught up in the infinity of it all.

You said we were stardust.

They were right,
you weren't to be trusted.
If only you could see
the irony in all your literary lies.
You're a slave to yourself.

If only you could see
the shame of you – perpetuating
a stereotype I'd never believed.
You let your father win.

This island brought you in
and yet you fear it. Fear us.
Poisoned by a Britishness
that doesn't become you.
Blind to the light – the war is over.
Nobody won.

They've made mockery of you.
You make mockery of life, of love,
consumed and dwelling on yourself.

You promised me the stars.

All hail the coward in you,
A stranger, a malevolence cast off
before fury caused real damage.

After all you said –
they were right.

On the Perils of Internet Dating

Almost by accident, the site appeared
and I jumped right in.
Sick of Sandinos' festooned walls,
its familiar, safe faces and DJ-rich halls.

Worth a try, I reasoned.
What's the worst that could happen?

Soon immersed in a snapshot stew,
I found there were too many smiles to take in.
Too many faces trapped inside, all anonymous,
and searching, just like me, all failing miserably.

Like a giant game of Guess Who.
Feeling trigger-happy, spoiled for choice,
then ruthless, when suddenly nothing appeals.
Cast out the undesirables in seconds.

Gone. In the flick of a mouse.
Besides the odd random compliment sent adrift,
though, typically, the handsome ones never reply.

If this *is* Guess Who, then the same rules apply,
and, to them, I'm just a face among many.
Another pawn in the game, a smile
among insincere smiles.

Two eyes and a mouth,
appealing.

The Digital Dilemma

We sat in silent fascination
as four-year-old fingers hovered
over a glossy magazine,
palms out, trying in vain
to magnify its photographs.

Have we come so far
that our young cannot distinguish
between hard copy and touchscreen?

Have we blurred so many lines,
Minority Report's sci-fi visions
are now real – and perfected by toddlers?

We couldn't help but stare, aghast
at how far we have fallen.
How our very notion of reality
distorts with progress.

She gave up, eventually,
having realised all efforts were futile,
and I set about explaining, yet again,
that paper isn't digital.

The Pocket Watch

Gripping it so tightly,
tiny, tender indentations
marked my palm
during the long walk home.

Fearful it, too, might vanish
– as he has.

Enveloped in a torrent of past,
I wandered. Bewildered.
Imagining my wedding day.
Who will give me away?

Its antiquated chain swayed
with every footstep, swinging time.
Full circle. Back home, where it began.

This delicate golden timepiece
chaining them, now left to me.

A gift, pressed into my hand
with whispered provenance.
A gift, as once my father gave it
to my grandfather, his elder.

Eyes on the road, head in the clouds,
I wandered
in the general direction of home.

Surrounded by ghosts –
though quite, quite alone.

The Comb

It was only a comb.
Narrow and brown, two for a pound –
but so sacred to me.

He used to keep it in his back pocket.
Tidy up the parting of his hair
should it go astray. He used
to stand there in front of the mirror.
Dedicated. Perfecting *The Look*.

And if he ever bent to lift things, the tip
of the shiny plastic would show. Sometimes
fall to the floor. Sometimes
I worried he would lose it.
He never did though. Reclaiming it
like a gold coin he'd just dropped.

It was just a comb …
Taking on a whole new meaning
now he has gone.
Significant
in its lasting insignificance –
still here, with no use.

Abandoned,
absentmindedly on a dashboard,
in a hire car,
a million miles away.

I lost my daddy's comb that day.

You Only Live Once

What does it mean? I asked,
presuming it might be French,
or some hip new language
too cool for us 'oldies' to use.

They scoffed at my ignorance
and giggled quietly under their breath
with all the defiance of youth.

Yolo … it rolled off my tongue
and left a sweet, buoyant taste,
– all for nothing.
Just another acronym, they said with glee.
Another lazy waste of words
and reason to **L**augh **O**ut **L**oud
for earth's illiterate future.

They cared nothing
for its lovely Latin equivalent
or the gusto with which
I blurted it out – *Carpe diem!*
Unimpressed, they rolled their eyes
and turned back to the TV.

If I'd had a dictionary at hand,
I'd have thrown it aloft
and willed its words to flutter down
settling deep on each of them.

Instead I, bemused,
and somewhat confused,
gave up 'til another day.

Unheard Voices

We work with the warmth of Ireland,
and, on occasion, are invited to share in
the hearths and hearts of its people.

We are strangers, yet they radiate sincerity.
They invite us in and warm us with tea,
sometimes offer a biscuit or two. I never do.
Too polite to make crumbs in conversation.

We invite words to flow, thoughts and memories,
and if they talk, they talk of their lives, of family,
of loss, of the appalling things they saw
when this country was at war.

Sometimes they share secrets, in the hope
we might make sense of them when they cannot.

We just listen. Caught up, we rise and fall
in the breath of others. With the gentle, the honest,
the burdened few who dare to speak aloud.

For days and weeks, we carry their words inside.
Weighed down by empathy, we learn from them,
allowing their imprint upon us.

Entrusted with the beautiful lives of others,
and made a storyteller, I am privileged.

For when we are gone,
our stories live on, taking flight.

Send-Off

(For Dee Canning)

Deep in the earth he now lies.
Devoid of the life so abundant
beneath frost and flowers.

It began at ten. I arrived at ten-past.
Sneaked in with an agitated blush,
rushed to the nearest vacant pew.
Disturbed total strangers –
shuffling in awkwardly.

Perched on the end of a row;
out on a limb, craved familiar face
or compassionate look. None came.
Air of disbelief; grief;
still seeing his face. Still hearing that
deep, raspy chuckle we'd grown accustomed to.
Too young to die. Too soon.
Too many young people gathered,
heads hung, hearts heavy with loss,
and I remember the priest made us laugh.

The date escapes me,
though I recall the black clothes;
black clouds; black moods; anger.
Bowed heads and ashen pale faces.
Make-up forming tiny, tearful rivulets
down carefully applied disguises.

Often we had worried for his welfare.
Often imagined the time would come
when he would no longer be.
Fragility never conquered;
grateful for all – he embraced.
Though slight, he stood mighty.
An exuberance now understandable.
A demise more certain than most.

Deep in the earth he now lies.
I suspect it was winter; December perhaps.
The wind cut deep through the mourners
lining the path; reluctant guard of honour.
Too frightened to laugh,
too nervous to cry.
We said goodbye.

Long Live the Compilation

I'll fight your corner 'til the end, old friends!

Still lost in your reverie, I'll take it on the chin,
refuse to move with the times. You're worth it.

Now you are subject to heated debate,
on the nights we have friends round and sit up late,
often discussing my fine audio array.

How can I cast you asunder now?

Nothing can compare to your sentiment.
Once all the rage, now unloved by most,
miniature storybooks detailing yesterday's dream.

I still extol your virtues to all who will listen
and stroke your kaleidoscope spines.

I still listen and learn, sing like no-one's listening,
head-spun as you chronicle the decades.

Consider the joys in someone's spent hours,
pouring over music, lining up just the right songs,
in just the right order *for your listening pleasure*.

Hearing old voices in handwritten track lists,
in tiny drawings, love notes, condensed proposals,
each one so intricate and idiosyncratic.

What's not to love? Surely they must admire
the dedication in maintaining now defunct delights?

Consider the rapt attention to detail.
The effort long-since discarded in the age of CD,
though that, too, has now died its death.

Still, I hold tight to those old battered tapes.

Row after row, petite, painted reminders
of all whom I loved. All who loved me back,
and made me a mix-tape to show it.

The Wild Atlantic Way

Take me down the Wild Atlantic Way
away from the daily grind, the transgressions
of this love-locked island, wanting.

Let's take your car and just go.
See the sights. Revel in Ireland's beauty, all her
rugged grace, forget the ties that bind and cut us deep.

Let's go and find ourselves.

We could leave from here. Take in the familiar
shores of Buncrana, Bundoran, Sligo, Galway,
and on, through the unknown.
Where land and sea collide.

Let's go all the way. Follow the winding coast
from Donegal down to Cork,
stopping only for sustenance
and for soft, sweet love in seaside B&Bs.

Let's go today, get away from here.
Flee; come back revived.

Late One Night …

… while the house was quiet,
I unearthed the stash of shopping bags
awaiting Christmas wrap, and searched.
Eager to see them again, up close.

They smiled at me, pristine in the box.

The ten-year-old in me was spellbound,
hooked on this tiny line-up of suspects,
so dainty, so hardy, well crafted.
Feeling giddy and tearful, I missed
the doll's house I never had.

A custom-built home
in which these toys could live,
and come alive at night
like they do in the movies.

The 36-year-old in me laughed off this lunacy,
the abrupt, irrational tears, the thrill,
the joy in stroking woollen hair
and giving each a name. I missed
the purity of childhood.

Filling the sink with water for the dishes,
I carefully put the little wooden family away
and got washing. Glasses first.

To Absent Friends and Bookends

I send up a kiss in the hope it arrives
caught on a breeze, soaring high
to those already lost.

There through years, all the constants
who kept my feet on the ground.

To you, my friend, whose laugh lit up a room
in sonic boom, we'll remember.

To you, my kin, conquered too soon,
we still talk to you, pine for you.

To you, my first squeeze, flying high
on that breeze, I'll always remember.

And when I can, I kiss
the bookends of life still surrounding,
the finest family and friends.

I shower them with swathes of love,
or at least I should – for it is they
who strengthen and sustain.

It is they
who toast my tiny successes
and hold me steady should I fall.

Visions of Auschwitz – 70 Years On

How many risked bullets and gas
to scribble vague lines among the detritus?

Desperate to leave faint hint of themselves
on parchment scrap, toilet paper, graffiti wall,
their lament buried deep in glass bottles.
Left to languish.

Under mass ashen graves
they found notebooks and diaries.
The *Sonderkommando's* paltry busts
– wrapped for the elements
and carefully placed beneath the bodies.

Knowing certain death was nearby,
Salman Gradowski scratched around in the dirt,
burying testimony of the tragedy surrounding.

Beneath the twisted sea of limbs
no longer human.
The perverse waxy despair
of the purged.

Dear Finder, search everywhere
in every inch of soil.

I cried at his decaying words of warning,
and that they had survived so much horror
when he had not.

A testament of evil, a lesson for love
we long should have heeded …

May the future judge us on the base of my notes
and may the world see in them, if only one drop, the
minimum of this tragic world amidst which we had lived.

Closing my eyes, I heard six million ghosts cry
and wondered if we'd learnt anything at all.

All Roads

Forget the world surrounding,
all the pitfalls sent to maim.
All the flights of fancy, hasty romances,
the mooned midnight dances.

I'm on a perpetual quest for more.

Forget always seeing beyond.
See now. See today.

Now is the time to breathe, let go
Celebrate myself. Seek no solace in others
but comfort from within.

Now is the time for vision. To take stock
of all I possess and the majesty created.

Now is the time to focus within.
Make more of me. Learn the lessons taught.
Enjoy motherhood more; be a dutiful daughter,
better friend than a lover. Reach out to
share all this happiness bubbling
just beneath the surface.

Forget the television.

Delve into the mountain of wrinkled pages
that masquerade as modern poetry.
Years of disarray demanding attention,
in need of tender gaze, of gentle stroke.
Now my words should shine.

All roads lead me here,
to this place, to this time.

Right now, in this hour –
the world is mine.

Praise for *Milk Teeth*

Julieann Campbell's *Milk Teeth* offers an arc of poetic power and nuance: there are tender moments, poignant truths, philosophical musings, stages of life and love, joy and sorrow. This is a collection that shimmers with the natural energy of illuminating reflection and universal truth. This is a poet comfortable with her craft.

The words of the poems are often rooted in lived experience and the echoing of memory – yet memory is never allowed to anchor the poems in nostalgia or melancholy. These poems may be understood more as open windows onto a life lived: where traces of nostalgia and melancholy swirl in poetic union with love, lineage, place, pride, sorrow, strength, and truth – as all gather together to give living form to both the past and the present.

Fittingly, the collection opens with *Trapped in Videotape* and *A Box-load of Memoirs*, works that contemplate how often all our pasts lie covered in the old dust of forgotten days. One of the true wonders of this collection is Campbell's ability – or more, her mission – to breathe life into memory and moments long past, so that they dance before us in the full awakening of the living poetry.

Place and time are key themes too. Campbell's home town of Derry – its past, its present, and its influence upon the poet – has a powerful presence and a grounding hold on the work so that the intimacy of the poetic expressions radiates through the universal truths on display. That influence may be recognized even when the work offers poetic journeys into the wider world or the thematic spectrum of the human story.

Campbell's poetic mode is to not burden her work with didactic reasoning nor to weigh the poems down with unnecessary anchors of melancholy or regret. But rather, with compelling honesty, *Milk Teeth* cuts with the precision and incision of a poet in full command of her art into the heartland of personal and universal truth

Take a journey through the word-scape of this, Julieann Campbell's stunning debut collection, and rest for a while in the refreshing honesty of the poems you will read and meet.

Dr Liam Campbell
(Ulster University)

An important debut collection from one of Ireland's finest young poets, emotionally intense, spiritually generous, lyrically beautiful … illuminating, at times prompting, provoking, inspiring … truly one to treasure.

Felicity McCall
(Author, founder of Derry Writers' Group)